SOUTHWARK

THE TWENTIETH CENTURY

The Globe Theatre, 1999. The present Globe Theatre owes its existence to Sam Wanamaker (1919–93), who pursued his dream of building a replica of Shakespeare's Globe for over forty years. By the time he died, it was well on the way to fulfilment. His architect was Theo Crosby (1925–94), who painstakingly recreated the 'wooden O' from all the best historical evidence, and who also designed a remarkable group of surrounding buildings with agreeable Classical details, a great rarity in modern Southwark. The buildings include an indoor theatre called the Inigo Jones Theatre. The excellent riverfront site of the new Globe is near the location of Shakespeare's Globe, which was in Park Street, just east of Southwark Bridge Road. The original Globe was part of an extraordinary flowering of playhouses in late Elizabethan London. The first playhouse was built in 1576 at Shoreditch across the river by James Burbage. He called it the Theatre. His sons, Cuthbert and Richard, had difficulty with their landlord after their father's death. They dismantled the building and re-erected its timbers in Southwark, where it was reopened in 1599 as the Globe. The Burbages owned one half of the business; the other half was held by five shareholders, one of whom was William Shakespeare. He was a member of the Lord Chamberlain's company, which exclusively occupied the Globe in its early years. Most of his plays were first performed there.

SOUTHWARK
THE TWENTIETH CENTURY

STEPHEN HUMPHREY

SUTTON PUBLISHING

First published in the United Kingdom in 1999 by
Sutton Publishing Limited · Phoenix Mill
Thrupp · Stroud · Gloucestershire · GL5 2BU

British Library Cataloguing in Publication Data
A catalogue record for this book is available from the British Library.

ISBN 0-7509-2409-8

Front endpaper: Queen Victoria's Diamond Jubilee procession passes the Obelisk in St George's Circus, Southwark, 22 June 1897. This photograph brings to the fore many aspects of turn-of-the-century Southwark: crowded streets, royal pageantry, a reflection of the British Empire at its high noon, and a huge inheritance of generally agreeable buildings from Georgian times. St George's Circus as seen here dated from the early 1800s; the last precious part of it to survive is that on the right-hand side. The procession is entering St George's Circus from Borough Road. A little way back on the left there may be seen a large viewing stand on the site of Borough Road Library (see page 79). Fees charged on that day partly paid for the library.

Half-title page: Southwark Park Road, *c.* 1928. It served as Bermondsey's main shopping street and incorporated a flourishing street market. In the days before this district became a fully developed suburb, the road was known as Blue Anchor Road, after the public house which still stands amidst the shops.

Title page: Michael Faraday (1791–1867) was a foremost son of Southwark. He was born in Newington Butts at the Elephant and Castle and originally served as a bookbinder's apprentice. He then became a laboratory assistant at the Royal Institution under Sir Humphry Davy, and later rose to be director of the laboratory. His principal achievement was the discovery of electromagnetism. In the twentieth century a street, a school and a memorial library (in Newington Library) have been named after him in Southwark (see page 38).

Back endpaper: A party from W.H. Wilcox & Co. Ltd, engineers' merchants, about to set off from Southwark Street to go to the Royal Windsor Show, August 1939. The firm had been established in 1878 and had extensive premises in Southwark Street. A hose factory was located in Canvey Street and later in Bankside. The premises seen here were destroyed in the Second World War.

TM ALAN SUTTON™ and SUTTON™ are the
trade marks of Sutton Publishing Limited

Typeset in 11/14pt Photina.
Typesetting and origination by
Sutton Publishing Limited.
Printed in Great Britain by
The Bath Press, Bath.

Contents

The Jolly Sailor, Lower Road, Rotherhithe. A maritime public house for a maritime district. For some centuries, Rotherhithe was noted for its shipbuilding, ship-repairing, shipbreaking and cargo-handling. Ships were built there for the Royal Navy and for the Honourable East India Company in some numbers in the eighteenth and early nineteenth centuries. From an earlier age, the master of the *Mayflower*, Christopher Jones, is buried in St Mary's churchyard. The earlier twentieth century saw the heyday of the Surrey Commercial Docks and of the riverside wharves. Cunarders of 14,000 tons plied from Greenland Dock between the wars, and the trade in timber and foodstuffs employed large numbers. No fewer than about 125 pubs were on hand to slake the workers' thirst; the late Cornelius Delay listed them and researched their histories. The Jolly Sailor, last rebuilt in about 1891, stood in Lower Road next to the former Town Hall and opposite St Olave's Hospital. All three buildings have now gone.

Introduction

The Mayor of Southwark for 1999–2000, Councillor Charles Cherrill, has adopted pride in the borough as the theme for his mayoralty. This book has a similar purpose, for it illustrates a borough whose history compares proudly with that of any part of London beyond the City, to which it was the first suburb as far back as Roman times. The book does not purport to be a history of Southwark, nor even a history of Southwark in the twentieth century. Instead, it shows through its illustrations numerous aspects of change which have loomed large in the economy, housing, social life and government of the area over the past 100 years. It is selective, because the pictures available inevitably tell us more of the changing townscape than anything else. There are emphases on the borough's economy, which is so often neglected but which is central to its history; and on its lost architectural highlights, which might prompt the securing of what we have left as an essential part of pride in the borough.

The twentieth century began on 1 January 1901, and just three weeks later there occurred the death of Queen Victoria, the great matriarch and symbol of nineteenth-century England. In London's local government, too, the new century brought a substantial change. The civil parishes which had governed locally since Tudor times were superseded late in 1900 by the new Metropolitan Boroughs of Bermondsey, Camberwell and Southwark. It was the merger of these three in 1965 which created the present London Borough of Southwark. The boroughs which were formed in 1900 established strong identities and loyalties. Civic pride flourished markedly in Edwardian times and the old photographs seem to say that the new Mayors and Aldermen considered their offices as a promotion and a privilege: a share in a proud Empire. Bermondsey's hold on its citizens was particularly strong. Camberwell's remit was inherited directly from a single civil parish, which allowed for almost complete continuity. Only in the old town of Southwark was there an obvious discontinuity, for the historic centre of the town was split (ridiculously) between the Metropolitan Boroughs of Bermondsey and Southwark.

The economy of Southwark at the beginning of this century was very different from what it is today. The riverfront from Blackfriars to Rotherhithe was a major part of the Port of London. The Surrey Commercial Docks, one of London's several systems of enclosed wet docks, occupied the greater part of the Rotherhithe peninsula, and wharves lined most of the riverside even above London Bridge. Ships voyaged across the world to bring goods to quaysides in this borough. Timber from the Baltic and from Canada came to Rotherhithe, where sheds and wharves for its storage abounded; and some of it was taken by barges along the Surrey Canal to Camberwell and Peckham, where there were many more timber yards. In the 1930s, huge 14,000-ton Cunarders plied between

Canada and the Greenland Dock at Rotherhithe, at the same time as small sailing ships brought timber from Finland. Foodstuffs came in great quantity to the borough's quays. Hay's Wharf and Butler's Wharf, which together occupied most of the riverfront from St Saviour's Dock upstream to London Bridge, were very significant businesses in the import of food. Tooley Street came to be called 'London's larder' and was the focus of the provision trade until well after the Second World War. It was characteristic of the district that a history of St Olave's Church in Tooley Street was written by an official of New Zealand's Department of Agriculture, who inspected imported butter.

Food processing was a major industry in Bermondsey. Some of the most familiar names in their fields ran factories there: Peek, Frean's for biscuits; Hartley's for jam; Crosse and Blackwell's for tinned food; Pearce, Duff's for blancmange and custard powder; and Courage's for beer. Brewing was a traditional riverside industry in many parts of London. Allied to it in Southwark was the hop trade, whose warehouses were a notable feature of Borough High Street and its vicinity. Leather manufacturing, hatmaking and engineering were further prominent local industries. The leather firm of Barrow, Hepburn and Gale made a sufficiently significant contribution to military supplies in the Second World War to prompt Field-Marshal Montgomery to visit the Grange Mills and to address the workforce. In hatmaking, Christy's of Bermondsey Street made hats for the Tower of London's Beefeaters and Mr Bowler himself once operated in Southwark Street. Among engineering firms, Hayward's of Union Street in Southwark made most of the coal hole covers in London; before the 1960s, coal was still a major domestic and industrial fuel. The firm of Kirkaldy's in Southwark Street had a world-wide fame for its expertise in testing materials for use in engineering projects.

The population of Southwark in 1901 was nearly three times as large as it is today. In the census of that year, the Metropolitan Borough of Camberwell had 259,000 people, which is the equivalent of a major provincial city such as Leicester. There was a slight decline throughout the borough down to 1939, but the vibrancy of the local economy maintained stability. New housing estates on the fringe of London and the opening of the Northern Line to Morden in 1932 led to a limited exodus. The parish magazine of St Mary, Newington, reported in 1936 that a good many parishioners had removed from Walworth to Morden in the recent past. But none of this was comparable with the huge dispersal of population brought about by the Second World War. Many families remained in new homes outside the borough after 1945. Industry and commerce within the borough did continue after the war, but by about 1960 closures and removals had begun. With the industry went the people, and there were great falls in population in the 1960s and 1970s. New housing on old industrial sites such as the Surrey Commercial Docks and the Bricklayers' Arms goods yard has since led to a modest rise.

Why did industry decline? Transport was a problem for some forms after the war. Local factories had been built in narrow streets in the days of horse-drawn traffic, and they found themselves badly sited when articulated lorries became normal. A site near the M4 became more attractive than one in Spa Road or Tooley Street. The Port of London moved downstream in the 1960s and 1970s when containerisation of cargoes was introduced. Ships became too big to unload in the Upper Pool or even at Rotherhithe, and appropriate quayside facilities were wanting. The decline of the upstream port left high and dry the factories which had been supplied from the upstream docks and riverside wharves. Thirdly, mergers and takeovers led to many closures. Local factories were almost always closed when their firms became parts of larger concerns. The great breweries of Barclay & Perkins and Courage provide good examples. Furthermore, local authorities were often remarkably anti-commercial in their attitudes. In the 1940s, the London County Council even went so far as to consider the forced removal of a major part of the leather industry from Bermondsey. It seems incredible that a public authority could even think of forcing out a major pillar of the local economy. No doubt, there was also a bandwagon effect from removals and closures. Local industry hardly existed by the end of the 1980s: a dramatic change from half a century before, and one of the most considerable changes in Southwark's history.

At the beginning of the century, most people lived in Georgian and Victorian terraced houses, or in late Victorian tenement blocks. Owner-occupation was almost unknown. Properties were rented from freeholders or leaseholders, who lived elsewhere. The vast majority of the properties were grouped into private landed estates, which had descended in family or institutional ownership from the eighteenth century or sometimes earlier. The Carr-Gomm Estate in Rotherhithe, the West Estate in Bermondsey and the Rolls Estate in Walworth, Camberwell and Bermondsey were all examples of the type. Their lands were largely first developed in the early nineteenth century by being leased to builders, who laid out the familiar streets. Estates of rented houses remained normal until the 1950s and 1960s, when they became uneconomic and were sold, often to local councils. The West Estate lasted until 1960, and the Rolls Estate until the death of Lady Shelley-Rolls in 1961, although in both cases there had been some earlier disposals. Commercial properties on old estates had tended to be sold between the wars. Big firms such as Bevingtons & Sons and Butler's Wharf typically bought their freeholds around 1930. Previously, they had leased them. Landed estates were conservatively run, which meant that little rebuilding took place. Properties got older and in need of more repair. The Second World War also damaged a great many of them. At the same time, the Rent Acts restricted income. Tenements fared worse than houses and often became notorious slums.

Council housing went back to the turn of the century, when the London County Council, the City Corporation and the civil parishes all began small developments. Between the wars, councils undertook bigger schemes, although only in Bermondsey was the scale of building notably large. After the Second World War, and especially after private housing estates had largely disappeared, the pace of redevelopment became huge. The plans contemplated in the 1960s were on a scale which was ultimately unsustainable. The horrors of such estates as the Aylesbury, the Heygate and the North Peckham date from that time. In addition, although some of the old property (for example, near the New Kent Road) had to be replaced, many terraced houses could have been restored. The streets north of Southwark Park Road in Bermondsey have seen vast redevelopment, whereas those to the south are still largely Victorian.

In the last decade, most new housing for rent has been built by housing associations rather than borough councils. Schemes have been smaller and, on the whole, architecturally more agreeable. A more human scale has returned. Very recently, as a result of a special programme in the vicinity of Bellenden Road in Peckham, Victorian properties in Nigel Road, Relf Road and Ainsty Road have been transformed to make these streets look as neat as when they were new. If only Victorian Walworth and Victorian Bermondsey had been treated in the same way!

The borough's fabric changed little overall between 1901 and 1940, despite new council housing in Bermondsey. Hitler's Blitz and the postwar planners then brought about terrible destruction and social dislocation. The Elephant and Castle was heavily bombed, but the old vibrancy of shops, pubs, restaurants and entertainment was finally dissipated in the London County Council's megalomaniac scheme in the late 1950s. The whole had been a mosaic of small enterprises and a few larger ones, but the new scheme was alien in scale and outlook to what had enlivened the place in the past. The Bricklayers' Arms suffered similarly, and much of the heart of old Rotherhithe, and the back streets of Walworth and Peckham. History's verdict on postwar redevelopment will be severe.

Since the 1950s, immigration from the West Indies, the Indian sub-continent and from Africa had had a considerable effect on Southwark's population. The numbers were relatively small until after 1970, but are now huge. One result is that many local churches have become West Indian or West African. The old Borough Road Baptist Chapel, whose congregation had waned, is now the Deeper Life Bible Church; and the Welsh Presbyterians of Falmouth Road have been superseded by the Brotherhood of the Cross and Star. In Camberwell, the obscure Catholic Apostolic Church has become a Greek Orthodox cathedral because of Greek Cypriot immigration. On the whole, these migrant communities have been poor and have yet to have a wider influence in local life.

Historians look for patterns, and several patterns have been clear to see in the last years of this century. One is the conversion to flats or hotels of old commercial buildings. A government ministry (Alexander Fleming House), an engineering factory (Babcock's) and hop warehouses (in Maidstone Buildings) have been among the conversions into flats. The trend to build hotels is a very recent one and is linked to increased tourism near the river. In turn, tourism has been stimulated by new attractions such as the Globe Theatre, Vinopolis and by the publicity for the Tate Gallery's intended branch on Bankside. Another recent pattern is the closure of public houses and their conversion to houses and hostels. More regrettably, a few with historic names have continued in use under new names which have no local links. The Plough at Dulwich is a prominent example of that dismal trend. In shopping, supermarkets and warehouses with large car parks have won much ground from traditional high street shops. The Old Kent Road illustrates that pattern very well. As the century ends, Southwark seems to be filling the considerable gaps which the waning of its earlier predominant patterns has left in recent decades.

The Edwardian Age
& the First World War

The Alfred's Head Public House, Elephant and Castle. 1904. This building
had a prominent position on the corner of London Road and Newington
Causeway. Two years later the Bakerloo Line underground station was to be
a new and notable neighbour on the London Road side. Notice that the
pub's clock was made in Great Dover Street in Southwark: one small
indicator of local industry. Observe also that the newspaper placard refers
to the Russo-Japanese War. The Alfred's Head was closed on 16 December
1961, and it was demolished in 1962 as part of the London County
Council's megalomaniac redevelopment scheme.

The proclamation of King Edward VII's coronation outside Bermondsey Town Hall, Spa Road, 15 July 1901. The Mayor, Colonel Samuel Bourne Bevington (1832–1907), stands in the centre, behind four trumpeters from the local Volunteers, whom he had long commanded. They were members of the 3rd Volunteer Battalion, the Queen's (Royal West Surrey Regiment). This was the first public occasion when the Mayor and Aldermen of the new Metropolitan Borough had appeared in robes in a Bermondsey street. The bewhiskered Alderman on the left is John Dumphreys, whose distinctive political stance was that of a Conservative working man. He was briefly the Member of Parliament for Bermondsey in 1909–10. Next to him is the Town Clerk, Frederick Ryall, who read the proclamation.

Bermondsey Volunteers on the steps of the Town Hall, Spa Road, 1902. Although there is no evidence to hand, it seems likely that these Volunteers had returned from the Boer War in South Africa. The Mayor at the bottom of the steps is Alexander Burton (1902–3). On the right of the municipal party is Joseph Watson, who edited the *Southwark Annual* and the *Southwark and Bermondsey Recorder*.

16

The corner of Newington Causeway (left) and New Kent Road (right), c. 1910. On the left there are the premises of Isaac Walton & Co. Ltd, a department store which had superseded a business called Tarn's. Walton's and Tarn's were as big as West End department stores, with a huge number of assistants living on the premises. The building with a turret on the corner was the Rockingham Arms Public House, another substantial structure, which flourished despite the Alfred's Head and the Elephant and Castle being on opposite corners of the junction. Notice a No. 1 bus emerging from New Kent Road. Its route originally took it from New Kent Road to Cricklewood.

Standard VIb in St Mary Newington School, Newington Butts, 1913. The class mistress was Miss Holmes. This school was the oldest in Walworth; it originated in the early eighteenth century, when the district was still a rural one, just beyond London. The school's site in Newington Butts, next to the Metropolitan Tabernacle, was close to the ancient site of St Mary's Church. The school was eventually closed, and its site was used to build the Elephant and Castle Baths in 1978.

Palmer's, London Road, Elephant and Castle, 24 January 1904. This was a famous business, divided between two shops. One well-known performer at the South London Palace, George Chirgwin, regularly ended his turn by saying, 'I must go over and have a basin full at Palmer's'. In those days, you could also cross the road in a pea-souper to have a bowl of pea soup! This and the following three pictures were all taken by Ernest Milner for the Baker Street and Waterloo Railway, that is, the future Bakerloo Line, whose terminus was to be opened in London Road in 1906.

The other Palmer's in London Road, at No. 48, 14 February 1904. Tripe and onions came in 3*d*., 4*d*. and 6*d*. platefuls.

Shops in London Road, Elephant and Castle, 24 January 1904, next to the South London Palace, a famous music hall (on the left).

London Road, Elephant and Castle, 14 February 1904. The great 5/- sale was still rather expensive at that time.

George Conquest (1837–1901), actor-manager of the Surrey Theatre, Blackfriars Road, 1895. At the turn of this century, George Conquest was the licensee and manager of a theatre which has been called 'A Major London Minor' in the title of a recent book by William Knight. Conquest had taken the lease in 1881. In his earlier years, he had played the Artful Dodger in *Oliver Twist*; the dramatization of Dickens's novel (which was partly set in Southwark) was one of the Surrey Theatre's notable successes. George Conquest was commemorated in 1937 when Bath Street (off London Road) was renamed Conquest Street. The theatre itself was closed in 1934.

A municipal delegation at the Vestry Hall, Borough Road, Southwark, 23 June 1911. These dignitaries are awaiting King George V, during whose coronation drive through South London they were going to present an address. The Mayor of Southwark in 1910–11, Alderman Albert Wilson, stands third from the left, next to the Town Clerk. Two Aldermen and their wives accompany them. The building was formerly the Vestry Hall of the Parish of St George the Martyr, Southwark, which had become part of the Metropolitan Borough of Southwark in 1900.

A group outside St Mary's Church, Rotherhithe, *c.* 1900. The Reverend Canon Edward Josselyn Beck stands in the centre. He was the Rector of Rotherhithe from 1867 to 1907 and performed the valuable service of writing *Memorials to Serve for a History of the Parish of St Mary, Rotherhithe* (1907). He had seen many changes in Rotherhithe and recorded them for later generations. This photograph is a splendid period-piece in the history of an Anglican parish.

Colonel Samuel Bourne Bevington (1832–1907) was the head of Bevingtons and Sons, of Neckinger Leather Mills in Abbey Street, Bermondsey's foremost firm of leather manufacturers. From 1900 to 1902 he served as the Metropolitan Borough of Bermondsey's first Mayor. In this photograph, taken in the garden of his home at Sevenoaks, Kent, he is shown seated in the foreground (on the left, with a stick), wearing the Mayor's chain. A statue of him was unveiled in Tooley Street in 1911.

The clock tower, St George's Circus, 1907. Ever since St George's Circus had been laid out in the eighteenth century, Robert Mylne's Obelisk had stood in this spot. In 1905, however, the Obelisk was removed to the grounds of the Royal Bethlem Hospital (now the Imperial War Museum) to make way for this tower, which was the gift of William Bowland Faulkner and Frederick Faulkner, tobacco, cigar and cigarette manufacturers of Blackfriars Road. Jan F. Groll was the architect, and the cost of building was about £3,500. The tower was inaugurated on 15 July 1907, by Sir William Treloar, Lord Mayor of London. It was built of Portland stone and Cornish granite, rose to 70 ft in height and had a lamp at each corner held by a winged dragon. The tower lasted just 30 years, for it was removed in 1937 as an alleged obstacle to traffic. This was a preposterous reason, because the old Obelisk took up just as much space, and the present roundabout takes very much more. Today, Mylne's Obelisk once again presides over St George's Circus, which is a very agreeable revival.

The clock tower in the churchyard of St Mary Newington, Newington Butts. Although this photograph was taken in 1970, it naturally forms a pair with that of the tower in St George's Circus, for they were contemporaries and parallels. This tower was built in 1877–8 to the designs of Henry Jarvis & Son and at the expense of R.S. Faulconer. It was 100 ft high and was built in Bath stone. Its site had been that of the church of St Mary Newington down to 1876. The tower was demolished in 1971 when Southwark Council considered the cost of repair to be too high.

Manor Methodist Church in Galleywall Road was built in 1865–6 for the United Methodist Free Churches, an offshoot of the mainstream Wesleyan Methodists. It became part of the reunited Methodist Church in 1932. During the First World War, its minister, the Reverend W. Kaye Dunn, was notorious for his alleged German sympathies and was forced to leave. The church was bombed in 1940 and was rebuilt in 1955. It is about to be rebuilt again.

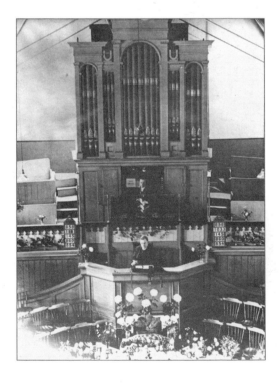

The interior of Manor Methodist Church, *c.* 1910. As in most buildings of the Free Churches, the preacher's pulpit dominates, and often (as in this case) the organ is sited behind the platform.

Almshouses, Lower Road, Rotherhithe, c. 1910. They were built in 1901 for seven married couples aged 60 or over under the will of Charles John Peele. He had been a partner in Brandram Brothers, a large firm of lead and paint manufacturers whose premises stood in Neptune Street on the other side of Lower Road. The trust was run by the Secretary of the firm until the works were closed in 1958. Henry Evan Brandram Peele, the son of the firm's senior partner, was ordained as an Anglican priest and became a curate of St Mary's, Rotherhithe, in 1902.

The Camberwell Home of the Aged Pilgrims' Friend Society in Sedgmoor Place, c. 1910. The society was founded in 1807 to help 'poor, aged and infirm Protestant Christians of both sexes'. Premises for 42 aged pilgrims were built in 1834–7 on a site given by William Peacock. He also established the Bethel Asylum in Havil Street in 1838. Camberwell and Peckham had many sets of almshouses, because they were seen in the early nineteenth century to be quiet and semi-rural areas away from the bustle of London. The premises were usually more ornate than ordinary houses, and fortunately most of them survive.

The garden of the almshouses in Sedgmoor Place has William Peacock's monument in the centre.

The funeral of eight boy scouts at St John's Church, Larcom Street, Walworth, 1912. The boys had drowned off Leysdown-on-Sea on the Isle of Sheppey on 4 August. The body of a ninth scout had not been found. A destroyer, HMS *Fervent*, had brought the bodies from Sheppey to Cherry Garden Pier in Bermondsey on 8 August. A procession had then been formed to St John's. On 9 August no fewer than 50,000 people visited the church to pay their respects. The funeral took place on 10 August and involved another procession from Walworth to Nunhead Cemetery, where the scouts were buried. The tragedy made a huge impression at the time. Rex Batten, a researcher on Nunhead Cemetery, has written a booklet on the subject in recent years and has reawakened interest in it on Sheppey and in Southwark.

The Mayor of Southwark, Walter C. Williams, heads this group at a horse parade outside Manor Place Baths in Walworth in 1912. Southwark Borough Council ran a depot in Manor Place, which required the services of a great many horses. Parades were held regularly, and people took much pride in turning out well-groomed horses, and also carts and harnesses in spotless condition.

The drawing room of Sir Henry Bessemer's mansion at Denmark Hill, *c.* 1910. Sir Henry (1813–98) was the inventor of a process of making steel. His estate at Camberwell, bought in 1863, boasted considerable grounds, an observatory and a farm. The mansion was called Bessemer House. After the Second World War, all this was cleared to make way for the Denmark Hill Estate. A similar fate befell John Ruskin's house next door, and the Kingswood Estate in the south of Dulwich. In all these cases, gracious Victorian properties and their grounds were lost.

An interior at the Grange, Grange Lane, Dulwich, *c.* 1900. The house was the home of Commander and Mrs Bailey, and the latter's sister, Mrs Atkinson, from 1890 to 1904. The house was bombed in the Second World War and has since been rebuilt.

Lance-Corporal Leonard James Keyworth VC is fêted at the Drill Hall in Walworth on 12 July 1915, after his investiture at Buckingham Palace by King George V. Although he came from Lincoln, he served in the 1/24th Battalion of the London Regiment, which was based at the Drill Hall in New Street (later renamed Braganza Street) in Walworth. Keyworth won his VC for an action at Givenchy, near Béthune in northern France, on 25–26 May 1915. He died of wounds on 19 October in the same year, aged 22, and was buried at Abbeville. In 1919 Dantzic Street at the Elephant and Castle was renamed Keyworth Street in his honour, and Faunce Street School later became Keyworth School.

During the First World War the 1/24th Battalion of the London Regiment, from Walworth, formed part of the 47th (London) Division on the Western Front. On 28 October 1918, the Band and Drums of the battalion led the division in a ceremonial entry into Lille in northern France after the retreat of Kaiser Wilhelm's army. Drum-Major W. Mew heads the procession. Posters set up in the city to welcome the division are among the records of the battalion which are now kept in Southwark Local Studies Library. The direct succession of units at the depot in Braganza Street came to an end in 1967. Major J.M.A. Tamplin wrote a substantial history of them in 1965, entitled *The Lambeth and Southwark Volunteers*.

King George V presents Able Seaman Albert Edward
McKenzie with the Victoria Cross, 1918. The recipient won
his honour when he served on HMS *Vindictive* in the
storming of the mole at Zeebrugge on 22–23 April 1918.
He died of influenza later in the same year, and is buried in
Camberwell Old Cemetery.

The Bermondsey and Rotherhithe War Memorial in West
Lane, Rotherhithe, photographed after its unveiling on 8
October 1921. It was not unveiled by a general or by a
government minister but by a local mother, Mrs Speer, who
had lost three of her sons in the First World War. The
principal speech at the unveiling was given by Arthur Carr,
the Chairman of Peek, Frean & Co. Ltd. The committee
which built the memorial also endowed a children's ward at
Guy's Hospital, which was dedicated on 7 February 1923.

The unveiling of the war memorial in West Lane, 1921. The preacher was the Reverend Canon J.C.V. Durell, Rector of Rotherhithe.

This monument was unveiled in what is now Old Jamaica Road in memory of members of the 22nd (County of London) Battalion, the London Regiment (The Queen's), who had been killed in the First World War. The unit was Bermondsey's principal contribution to the Territorial Army and was based in the Drill Hall on the corner of Abbey Street and Old Jamaica Road. Previously, the unit had been known as the 3rd Volunteer Battalion, the Queen's (Royal West Surrey Regiment) (see page 16). The Royal West Surrey Regiment was the parent regiment in the regular army, which had been formed to defend Tangier in the days of King Charles II. It was named after his wife, Queen Catherine of Braganza, because Tangier had been part of her dowry. Its badge, the lamb and flag, appears at the head of this monument.

Industry & Commerce between the Wars

Warehouse in Tooley Street, *c.* 1920. The northern part of the borough, especially near the river, possessed many huge warehouses in the days when the upstream Port of London was fully working. Cereals, hops and other foodstuffs were the most frequent items to be stored. Tooley Street became the centre of the provision trade. No. 68 Tooley Street, shown here, was occupied in 1920 by R.A. McCallum & Sons, provision merchants. Horse-drawn vehicles were still widespread between the wars.

The tanning shed at Bevingtons and Sons' Neckinger Leather Mills, Abbey Street, Bermondsey, June 1931. The word tanning derives from tannin, a constituent of oak bark, which has traditionally been used to harden hides and skins. The main building of this firm still stands next to the railway bridge in Abbey Street. The company ceased to operate there in 1982.

Tea being repacked for export, Hay's Wharf, Tooley Street, c. 1920. Tea had been a principal foundation of the firm's Victorian prosperity. An alliance between John Humphery, proprietor of the wharf from 1838 to 1863, and the great Far Eastern trading firm of Jardine, Matheson & Co., brought the famous China tea clippers to Southwark's waterfront. In the 1860s they would race with the new season's tea from Foochow to Southwark: a striking example of the upstream Port of London's ocean-going trade in its heyday. Today, a public house called the Horniman at Hay's occupies a former warehouse next to the old Hay's Dock to recall the tea trade. John Humphery served as an Alderman and Lord Mayor of London, and as the Member of Parliament for Southwark.

Tea being bulked at Hay's Wharf, *c.* 1920.

Hay's Dock earlier this century. Alderman Humphery had warehouses and a dock built in 1856–7 by the contractor, William Cubitt, to the designs of William Snooke and Henry Stock. It was this part of Hay's Wharf which housed the firm's tea trade, which was a central pillar of the business in Victorian times.

Mark Browne's Wharf, *c.* 1930. The ship in the picture was of the largest size which normally plied so far upstream. Notice the barges which surround it. Barges or lighters were very numerous in the old upstream Port of London. Cargoes were unloaded into them, for removal elsewhere in the port, as much as they were unloaded on to quays. Mark Brown's Wharf became part of Hay's Wharf's business in 1929.

The SS *Jasper* at Butler's Wharf near Tower Bridge, *c.* 1920. Butler's Wharf was a substantial business downstream of Tower Bridge. It dealt chiefly in foodstuffs.

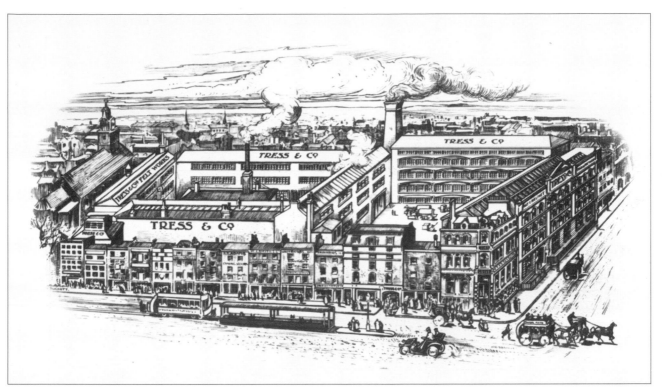

An artist's impression of the premises of Tress & Co., hatters, in the angle between Blackfriars Road and Stamford Street, Southwark. Sainsbury's subsequently occupied this property. The hatmaking industry in Southwark was split into two: one half was based in or near Bermondsey Street and the other around Blackfriars Road. This factory was possibly the largest in the local industry. (Sainsbury's Archives)

The Hop Exchange, Southwark Street, 1921. The damage shown in the picture had been caused by a fire on 20 October 1920. Subsequently, the top two storeys were removed and the rest was restored as offices. In its original state, the exchange resembled the Colosseum. It was built in 1866–7 to the designs of R.H. Moore. Although Southwark was undoubtedly the centre of the hop trade, there was probably no need for an exchange. The hop merchants in the district had substantial premises of their own. This is one of Southwark's most important nineteenth-century buildings.

Mansons Ltd, transport maintenance engineers, in Ingoldisthorpe Grove, Peckham, between the wars. The property on the left has fluted Ionic pilasters, which once appeared on a number of late Georgian and early Victorian houses in this area.

The workshop of Mansons Ltd.

Staff of Heinz & Co.'s factory at Peckham in June 1922. Howard Heinz (in the centre of the picture) took over the running of the company on his father's death in 1919. The Peckham factory was the company's first in England; the firm had bought the old-established pickle manufacturers, Batty & Co. of 127 Brayards Road. The premises included railway arches; 17 were used for storage. Although Peckham as a whole was largely a residential district, there was a sizeable industrial and commercial presence, chiefly near the Surrey Canal and in and near Rye Lane, Peckham High Street and Queen's Road.

Mill Street, Dockhead, Bermondsey. This street runs along the eastern side of St Saviour's Dock. At one time Bermondsey's mill stream ran along this street, on the right-hand side, and St Saviour's Mill occupied the site of Reed's Wharf. By the nineteenth century, the premises were largely commercial. The first Peek, Frean's biscuit factory was established on the left-hand side in 1857, and remained there until a fire destroyed it in 1873. The ingredients for the biscuits flowed out into the road and were famously baked all over it on that occasion. Peek, Frean's operated only in Drummond Road afterwards. Between the wars, Mill Street was one part of an almost solid wall of warehouses which lined the borough's waterfront. The enclosed wet docks have received much attention from historians, but the warehouses or wharves also played a prominent part in the Port of London in its heyday. The Southwark Local Studies Library holds property deeds for most of this street.

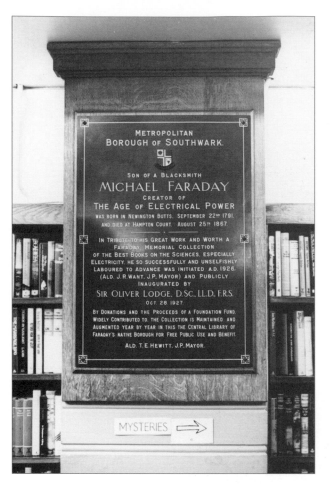

This plaque in Southwark Central Library, Walworth Road (Newington Library), commemorates the inauguration of a Faraday Memorial Collection by Sir Oliver Lodge in 1927. It was one of the various local tributes made to Michael Faraday earlier this century. Although Faraday was honoured chiefly as a scientist, it must be remembered that his achievements, and those of other pioneers and inventors, were of great *commercial* value. The economy of the borough was underpinned by such inventions as Bryan Donkin's tinning of food, Hayward's patent safety coal hole covers and ways of producing gelatin from unpromising materials. But Faraday's discoveries towered over all of them.

Walworth Road in the First World War. Retailing was an important part of the borough's interwar economy. Rye Lane in Peckham boasted the great department store of Jones and Higgins, which employed 1,000 people by the 1920s, and another large store called Holdron's. The Elephant and Castle was also a very significant place for shops, led by Tarn's (later Isaac Walton's), Rabbits' (for shoes) and Hurlock's. Quite significant retailing businesses existed in further main streets, such as Carter's in the Old Kent Road and the subject of this picture, Grose Brothers in Walworth Road. In almost all cases, businesses which were founded in the second half of the nineteenth century lasted until the Blitz. Some survived well after the Second World War, but the heyday of local retailing lasted from 1870 to 1940.

Housing between the Wars

Great Maze Court, Southwark, January 1939. This court of poor houses disappeared subsequently and became part of the site of Guy's Hospital. It lay east of Great Maze Pond. The building in the background is a hop warehouse. Bermondsey, Rotherhithe and Southwark had numerous enclaves of houses such as this, almost all of which were destroyed in wartime bombing or in postwar redevelopment. In the eighteenth century, Dr Johnson wrote: 'If you wish to have a just notion of the magnitude of this city, you must not be satisfied with seeing its great streets and squares, but must survey the innumerable little lanes and courts. It is not in the showy evolutions of buildings, but in the multiplicity of human habitations which are crowded together, that the wonderful immensity of London consists.'

St Mary's Place,
Rotherhithe, 5
February 1935.

Bantry Place,
Bermondsey, 1938.

Arnold's Place, Dockhead, Bermondsey, *c.* 1936. An advertisement for *The Labour Messenger* is fixed to the wall on the left. Notice, too, all the ground-floor shutters on the houses.

Grange Walk, Bermondsey. This street contains the oldest houses in Bermondsey and it has managed to survive through thick and thin. The house behind the lamp post incorporates in its fabric part of a mediaeval gatehouse of Bermondsey Abbey. The road went towards the abbey's grange or home farm.

Ainsty Street from Seth Street, Rotherhithe, January 1939. The almost total absence of vehicles is the most striking feature of these pre-war back streets to end-of-the-century eyes.

Bethel Place, off Vine Lane, Tooley Street, 1933. This area was almost entirely commercial, but a small pocket of housing managed to survive amidst the warehouses and factories until the 1980s.

Trinity Road, Rotherhithe, 1935. The Surrey
Commercial Docks can be seen in the
background. Trinity Road took its name from
Holy Trinity Church, which had been built on
the eastern side of Rotherhithe in 1838.

Victoria Place, 1934.

Wagstaff Buildings, Southwark, *c.* 1920. These weatherboarded houses in a narrow alley look even more fragile and poor than the brick-built Bermondsey ones.

The Mayor of Bermondsey, William Bustin, lays the foundation stone of flats in Silver Street, Rotherhithe, in 1922. The properties were the first to be built by Bermondsey Borough Council after the First World War. Councillor Bustin (1866–1957) served as Mayor in 1919–22. He was chiefly known for his work in the Bermondsey Gospel Mission, which he headed from 1891 to 1946 in succession to his father-in-law, Walter Ryall. His wife (on the right) was a Gospel singer, who was well-known as Madame Annie Ryall (1864–1950).

Wolseley Buildings at Dockhead, Bermondsey, were built in 1883. They were named after Field-Marshal Viscount Wolseley, a Victorian military hero, who had led the Ashanti expedition in West Africa in 1874 and the campaign in Egypt in 1882 which suppressed Arabi Pasha's revolt. In 1883, such tenements were seen as progressive, with better amenities and sound construction, but within about 50 years they had declined markedly. These tenements were all demolished after the Second World War.

Block 2 of the Harold Estate, Page's Walk, under construction, July 1934. Between the wars, Bermondsey Borough Council built a large number of blocks of flats to replace Victorian and earlier terraces. They changed the face of much of Bermondsey, and removed many old streets and alleys.

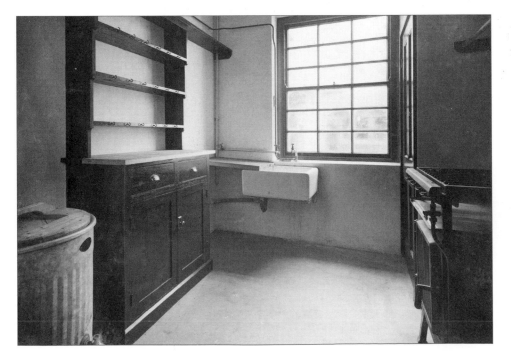

A 'kitchenette' on the new Harold Estate, August 1934.

Southwark Scenes & Southwark Folk between the Wars

Arthur Carr, the Chairman of Peek, Frean & Co. Ltd, at the opening of the joy slide in St James's Churchyard in 1922. He was the head of the great firm of biscuit manufacturers, which was one of the largest industrial concerns in Bermondsey. This dignified captain of industry nevertheless tried out the slide himself at the opening. W.J. Dixon of Blue Anchor Lane made the slide.

Alexandra Rose Day, 1938. Collectors are seen here on the steps of Bermondsey Town Hall, Spa Road, in the presence of Councillor Albert Mansell Downing, Mayor of Bermondsey. This was a popular observance associated with Queen Alexandra, the wife of King Edward VII. She had founded Alexandra Rose Day in 1912 to raise money for hospital patients. The day was held in June to commemorate her first landing in England from Denmark. Queen Alexandra died in 1925.

St Olave's Church, Tooley Street, *c.* 1925. The church in the picture was built in 1737–40 by Henry Flitcroft, who also designed St Giles-in-the-Fields near Charing Cross Road. Flitcroft's building had succeeded earlier ones whose origins went back to the eleventh century. St Olave's Parish, once very populous, became depopulated as commercial property took the place of houses, and the church was closed in 1918. In this photograph, it is advertised for sale. The church was demolished in 1926–8 and the site was subsequently used by Hay's Wharf to build a new headquarters called St Olaf House. The eleventh-century Norwegian king who gave his name to the church and the office block is depicted in an incised drawing and inscription on the latter today.

Class I of Melior Street Roman Catholic School, near London Bridge station, November 1932. The school has since been closed, but the Catholic church of Our Lady of La Salette and St Joseph still exists in Melior Street.

Unemployed men outside the Labour Exchange in Brunel Road, Rotherhithe, hearing of a 10 per cent reduction in unemployment pay, 1931.

Children from Monnow Secondary School in Bermondsey on a summer visit to Germany in 1930. It was highly unusual before the war for a school to run visits to the Continent.

Bermondsey Book Shop, 171 Bermondsey Street, 1927. Sidney and Ethel Gutman founded the bookshop in 1921 'to bring books and the love of books into Bermondsey'. It was first housed at No. 89 Bermondsey Street and later at the address shown here. It was more of a literary club and a mission than an ordinary bookshop, and many well-known writers of the time were invited to its meetings or were asked to contribute to its journal, *The Bermondsey Book*. This interesting by-way of literary history lasted until 1930.

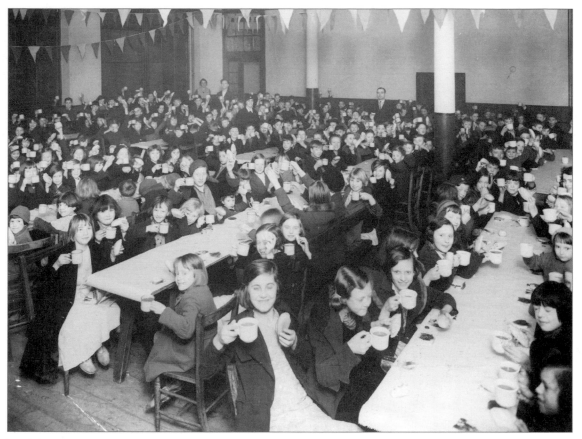

Breakfast for local schoolchildren at Bermondsey Central Hall, 1934. Between 300 and 400 children were given cocoa, and bread with jam or dripping, without charge. The Central Hall, which had been opened in 1900, was the principal Methodist church in Bermondsey.

The interior of Most Holy Trinity Church, Dockhead, Bermondsey, *c.* 1919. This Roman Catholic church of 1834–5 was destroyed in the Second World War and was subsequently rebuilt. The architect of this building was J.J. Scoles. A V2 attack on this church on 3 March 1945 killed three priests and led to a difficult operation to rescue a fourth. For his courageous part in the rescue, Albert Heming was awarded the George Cross.

Belair Farm, Dulwich, *c.* 1930. When industry and commerce were at their peak on the Bermondsey and Southwark waterfronts, Dulwich still had farms. Belair Farm in Gallery Road belonged at this time to Sir Evan Spicer, the paper magnate. After his death in 1938, the contents of the farm were auctioned, including 'an iron-grey cart horse' called Dobbin, ten Muscovy ducks and some Guernsey cattle.

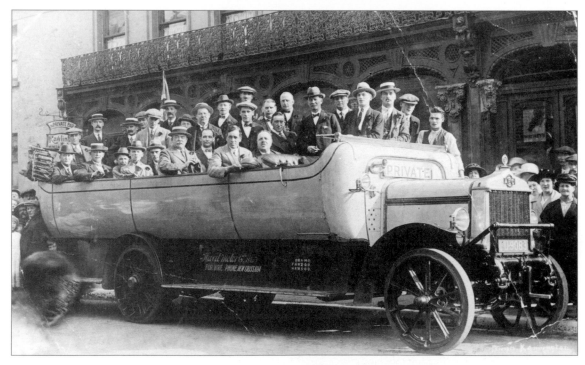

An outing from the Anchor and Hope Public House, Addington Square, Camberwell, 10 July 1921. The 'beano', usually starting from outside a public house, is a frequent subject among old local photographs.

The waiting room of the St Mary Newington Dental Department, 61 Penrose Street, Walworth, probably in the late 1920s.

Girl guides at Browning Hall, Browning Street, Walworth, 1927.

All Saints' School, Jesmond Street, Walworth, 1924–5. These boys were aged 9 and 10, and their schoolmaster was a Mr Clark. The school was associated with All Saints' Church, Surrey Square, an Anglican parish which no longer exists separately. Originally, just one church – St Mary, Newington – served the whole of Walworth, but by the beginning of this century there were 17 Anglican churches in the same area. Many of them have since gone.

The former All Saints' School building in Jesmond Street, 1964. The buildings were damaged by bombing in 1941 but lingered on in other uses for many years.

The opening of an extension to the slipper baths and laundry at Manor Place Baths, Walworth, 4 November 1933. Personal baths and public laundry facilities were just as important as swimming baths in these establishments earlier this century, whereas today they seem remarkable. Few people had their own facilities in the early 1900s. The Mayor in this photograph is Councillor P.M. Middleton.

A reception prepared for the Lord Mayor of London by the Mayor of Southwark at Manor Place Baths, February 1935. The baths' building was used for numerous civic and social occasions, and for other sports, especially boxing. The building was in use as baths and washhouses from 1898 to 1978, when it was superseded by a new building at the Elephant and Castle.

King George V and Queen Mary travel along Walworth Road during their Silver Jubilee Drive, 18 May 1935. In this photograph, they are passing the White Hart Public House and part of the extensive premises of William Hurlock. These premises were situated near the Elephant and Castle, in that part of Walworth Road where the Elephant and Castle Shopping Centre now stands. The alleyway seen here next to the White Hart was called Farrell Court. All the roads leading to the Elephant and Castle were lined with shops before the war. Bombing and postwar redevelopment destroyed the vibrancy of the old Elephant.

A fancy-dress party in St Matthew's Church Hall, New Kent Road, in the 1930s.

Municipal Endeavour between the Wars

Henry Syer Cuming (1817–1902), photographed in 1897. He lived at
63 Kennington Park Road, where he kept his substantial collection of
antiquities, curios, books, manuscripts and pictures. His father, Richard
(1777–1870), had been a collector before him. He bequeathed his
collections to the Metropolitan Borough of Southwark, and they were
opened to public view in Walworth Road as the Cuming Museum in
1906 (see page 63). Henry Syer Cuming was a Vice-President of the
British Archaeological Association and wrote copiously about objects
from all over the world. Without his family's keeping such daily
ephemera as advertisements, playbills, admission tickets and
programmes, we would know much less about nineteenth-century
Walworth. His museum was a major municipal institution between the
wars, and his old house became the basis at that time of the Southwark
and Lambeth Housing Society: a local example of a movement which
grew in various parts of London.

The heart of municipal Bermondsey, Spa Road, *c.* 1920. The taller building in the middle is the Town Hall of the Metropolitan Borough of Bermondsey. It had been built for a previous authority, Bermondsey Vestry, in 1880–2, at a cost of £60,000. Messrs. G. Elkington & Son were the architects. The building was bombed in the Second World War, and the last remains of it were cleared away in 1963. On the right there are the old baths and washhouses, which were built in the 1850s and preceded all other public baths in the present borough by a generation. They were replaced by new baths in Grange Road in 1927. The building in the background, beyond the Town Hall, is the former Bermondsey Library, which still stands but is now in use as offices. The library was opened in 1892 and became the central library of the Borough of Bermondsey in 1900. John Johnson was its architect. The library was closed in 1989, by which time Spa Road was a backwater.

Bermondsey Borough Council meeting in the large hall of the Central Library, Spa Road, 7 October 1930, during alterations to the council chamber in the Town Hall. The Mayor is Councillor George Stephen Tingle.

New municipal offices were built between the wars for Bermondsey Borough Council in Spa Road, at the junction with Neckinger, on the site of the original public baths. The offices were designed in Greek Classical style by H. Tansley, the council's architect. The foundation stone was laid on 20 October 1928, and the building was opened on 1 November 1930. When the old Town Hall was bombed in the Blitz, the new offices became the municipal headquarters for the Metropolitan Borough of Bermondsey.

The entrance hall of the new municipal offices in Spa Road.

Bermondsey Central Children's Library, January 1924. Early public libraries had often seemed rather forbidding places. In the 1920s changes were made to make them more open and attractive, and this included greater provision for children.

At the counter of Bermondsey Central Children's Library, January 1924.

In most of the postwar decades, the production of electricity was a state monopoly. But until 1948, electricity undertakings were often municipal, as this photograph of Bermondsey's Electricity Showroom in Lower Road, Rotherhithe, demonstrates. The council had an Electricity Committee which supervised the department.

The Stores Department of Bermondsey Borough Council, 1936. The council ran a great many operations from premises in Spa Road and Neckinger.

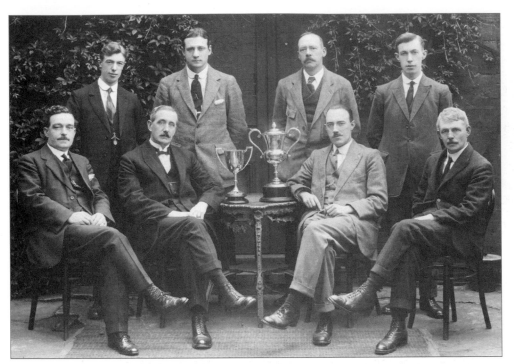

The Bermondsey Municipal Officers' Whist Team, 1922–3. The team had won the National Association of Local Government Officers' Metropolitan District Whist Cup and the Metropolitan Inter-Borough Whist Challenge Cup. The vast expansion of local government since the Second World War has made us forget that 70 or 80 years ago the status of a local government officer was far higher.

Workmen relaying Rotherhithe Street for Bermondsey Council in the late 1920s.

The Cuming Museum, Walworth Road, December 1921. The Cuming Museum was opened in 1906 in a specially-built extension to the public library in Walworth Road. The museum derived from the bequest by Henry Syer Cuming (1817–1902) of his collections, his house (63 Kennington Park Road) and an endowment. The result was not a museum of local history but a 'British Museum in miniature'. The first phase of the museum's existence was ended when it was bombed in 1941. It was not re-opened until 1959.

Distribution of money by the St Mary Newington United Charities, 1925. From the sixteenth century onwards, many individuals and institutions left money and property to local parishes for the relief of the poor and other charitable purposes. The endowments are still adminstered according to the old civil parishes, but usually in alliance with the borough council. In this case, the Town Hall of the Metropolitan Borough of Southwark was the former Vestry Hall of the Parish of St Mary, Newington. The Mayor in this picture is Alderman James R. Want.

An inspection of Southwark Council's horses at Manor Place Depot, *c.* 1920.

The last horse in the service of Camberwell Borough Council, March 1933. Many horses were once kept by the borough councils and by their predecessors, the vestries; it was as natural to have a Fodder Committee in 1900 as it is to have a Housing Committee today. Camberwell switched to motor vehicles relatively early.

The
Second World War

Wartime destruction at the Grange Mills of Barrow, Hepburn and Gale Ltd.,
Bermondsey, 1941. This major firm in Bermondsey's leather industry made
a significant contribution to military supplies during the war, and as a result
Field-Marshal Montgomery visited the firm on 30 March 1944.

During the Second World War, in 1944–5, water vans from Bermondsey saw active service in Normandy, Belgium and the Netherlands. They were used to keep down the dust on airfields and were operated by the 78th Road Construction Company of the 16th Airfield Construction Group of the Royal Engineers. The vans ended their days on an airfield at Volkel in the Netherlands, flying the flag for Bermondsey to the last. They had been built at the Neckinger Depot.

Bermondsey Wing of 409 Squadron, Air Training Corps, 1942.

Cadet David Eric Clowe, G.M., 1943. Cadet Clowe, of the Merchant Navy, was 19 years of age when he was awarded the George Medal for heroic devotion to duty after his ship had been torpedoed in the Atlantic Ocean. He was one of 38 men who drifted in a lifeboat and one of only seven who survived to be rescued; by then he had found himself in charge of the boat. He was given a sum of money and heard an official appreciation of his courage and endurance at a meeting of Bermondsey Borough Council in September 1943. Cadet Clowe lived in Thorburn Square, Bermondsey.

Members of the Women's Voluntary Service (later the WRVS) making camouflage in Bermondsey during the Second World War.

The piggery at Burtt's Yard, Albany Road, Camberwell, 1942. It was installed on a vacant piece of ground in the yard as a wartime measure. The firm was E.R. Burtt & Sons, builders' merchants. Burtt's dealt particularly in cement and ran Portland Wharf near Tower Bridge as well as the yard in Albany Road.

The Bermondsey Gospel Mission was open day and night during the Second World War as a shelter and a first-aid post. This photograph is of the basement shelter in 1941. The mission's building was located on the corner of Abbey Street and Old Jamaica Road, opposite the Territorials' Drill Hall.

Bermondsey Public Libraries' Shelter Service in the Second World War. There were 62 collections of books, and at the peak of the service, no fewer than 6,000 books were on loan.

Bomb damage in Lower Road, Rotherhithe, September 1940. Southwark Park Methodist Church stands on the left. It was a casualty of the war and was demolished some years later. The Blitz began on 7 September 1940, and affected this area severely as it was adjacent to the Surrey Commercial Docks. The topography of this area was much altered by the new roundabout in 1979, which removed the line of road seen in this picture. As in so many areas, postwar planners have knocked the life out of localities they have touched. The postwar destruction in Lower Road and Jamaica Road and in adjoining parts of old Rotherhithe was particularly severe.

St Mary Magdalen's Church, St Mary's Road, Peckham, after bombing, 1940. Four people were killed when the building was hit on 21 September. The church had been built in 1839–41 to the designs of Robert Palmer Browne at a cost of £4,309. The agreeable nineteenth-century Gothic structure was replaced in 1961–2 by a gaunt and stark modern design by the firm of Potter and Hare (see page 85). The new, cruciform building cost £65,000.

Grenard Road, Peckham, apparently a VE Day party, 1945. Street parties in Southwark were numerous for the Silver Jubilee of King George V in 1935, for the Coronations of 1937 and 1953, and for VE Day. A few were arranged for the present Queen's Silver Jubilee in 1977.

Percy Clare, MBE, Chief Librarian in the Metropolitan Borough of Bermondsey, 1950–65, photographed in October 1956. During the Second World War he served as the borough's Deputy Food Officer, for which service he was awarded the MBE.

The Grange, Bermondsey, 1948. Prefabs were a long-lasting result of the Second World War. Although they were intended to be temporary, a large number survived for a generation, and some still stand today.

The interior of a prefab at 118 Abbey Street, Bermondsey, 1946. The upright piano is a surprising item to present-day eyes, but they were far more numerous earlier this century than they are today. One old photograph of Peckham High Street shows two different piano shops side by side, whereas today such shops are unknown in the borough.

Postwar Public Libraries

The Old Kent Road Library, 1955. This building stood at the junction of
Old Kent Road and New Kent Road until 1968. It had been built for the
Metropolitan Borough of Southwark in 1907–8 to the designs of Claude
Batley, and it was the most architecturally distinguished library in the
present borough. This excellent building, a boon and an ornament to the
borough, fell victim to the Bricklayers' Arms flyover scheme which has
disfigured the district for the past 30 years.

As soon as local public libraries were founded in the late nineteenth century, they began to collect materials on the history of their districts. Only after the Second World War, however, did the subject of local history expand markedly. Bermondsey Public Libraries had a well-stocked and well-indexed local collection in the borough's central library in Spa Road, photographed here in 1951. After the three boroughs of Bermondsey, Camberwell and Southwark were merged, a Southwark Room was established in 1967 in Newington District Library in Walworth Road to hold a collection for the entire borough (see below).

The Southwark Room at Newington District Library, 1978. The local history collection of the London Borough of Southwark was housed here from 1967 to 1978, following the merger of the three Metropolitan Boroughs and their separate collections. Miss Mary Boast, the first Local Studies Librarian, is on the right. She wrote all but one of the eight *Neighbourhood Histories* which appeared in the 1970s and 1980s. For all her efforts in local history over 40 years, she was awarded the Freedom of the Borough in 1994. The local history collection moved to 211 Borough High Street in 1978, where it is still housed.

Postwar Change for Southwark's Churches

All Souls' Church, Grosvenor Park, 1970. The church dated from
1870–1 and served the southern end of the old parish of St Mary,
Newington. It was demolished in 1974 and its site was used for a block
of flats. H.Jarvis & Son designed the church. The firm was responsible for
many buildings in Victorian Walworth.

The Welsh Presbyterian Chapel, Falmouth Road, New Kent Road. It was built in 1888–9 to the designs of W. Charles Evans and was one of several Welsh churches founded in South London in the nineteenth century. The Welsh Presbyterians formerly called themselves Calvinistic Methodists. Before going to Falmouth Road, they had used a chapel in Crosby Row, Bermondsey, which had been built for John Wesley, the founder of the Methodist Church, in the eighteenth century. The reduced congregation in recent times led to the relinquishment of the Falmouth Road building in 1982. It was taken over by the Brotherhood of the Cross and Star. The growth of West Indian and West African congregations in Southwark has been a notable trend in the past 30 years. Today, when so many of them appear to flourish, there is only one Welsh-speaking congregation left: the one which meets in the Welsh Congregational Chapel in Southwark Bridge Road.

Holy Trinity Church, Trinity Church Square, 1960. This church was built in 1823–4 to the designs of Francis Bedford to serve as a daughter-church of St Mary, Newington. At that time the ancient parishes were becoming very populous and required more churches. St Peter's in Walworth, St George's in Camberwell and St James's in Bermondsey were all contemporary with Holy Trinity Church. This church was closed in 1959 and following fire damage in 1973, it was refitted as a rehearsal hall for the London Philharmonic and London Symphony Orchestras under the name of the Henry Wood Hall. This church was the original of Tom Costello's song, 'At Trinity Church I met my doom' (that is, made a bad marriage). A well-known statue of King Alfred, which stands in front of the church, has lately been proved to have come from the mediaeval Westminster Hall.

Morning prayer in St Mary Magdalen's Church, Bermondsey Street, 1961. This is one of Southwark's ancient parish churches which has survived wars and fires, and amidst the catalogue of demolitions which this chapter presents, it is pleasing to report that this church still ministers to the local population as it did in the Middle Ages. Originally, it was the parish church at the gates of Bermondsey Abbey. The present church building dates from 1677–80 and was designed by Charley Stanton.

Most Holy Trinity Church, Dockhead, Bermondsey, 1961. This postwar rebuilding of a bombed Roman Catholic church, by H.S. Goodhart Rendel, is one of the more interesting modern churches of the borough. Its twin towers and huge arches seem to echo Norman buildings. As a result of the new Jamaica Road being laid out to join Dockhead in the early 1960s, the church ended up with an uncommonly fine site. Goodhart-Rendel had also designed St Olaf House, the headquarters of Hay's Wharf, between the wars.

St Mary Magdalene's Church, St Mary's Road, Peckham, c. 1972. To a traditionalist, the design of postwar churches is usually disagreeable. It needs to be emphasized how cheap it was to build even the largest church in Victorian times, and how expensive it has become since 1945 even to repair a small church. Consequently, so many postwar churches can seem gaunt and stark. It was also the case that architectural fashion in the 1950s and 1960s eschewed ornament and any hint of the Gothic and Classical past.

The cargo in the previous picture is shown here being taken off a ship alongside Mark Browne's Wharf, 1958. The white building across the river with the columns is the Custom House in the City of London. This part of the river, the Upper Pool, was the heart of the old upstream Port of London. The fact that Tower Bridge was built as a bascule bridge in the late nineteenth century was due to the many ships which needed to reach the Upper Pool.

Willson's Wharf, c. 1958. This wharf was part of the Hay's Wharf empire and was situated near Battlebridge Lane off Tooley Street. It handled at various times coffee and cocoa, dried fruit and provisions, and wines and spirits.

The former premises of Harland and Wolff Ltd, Finland Yard, Redriff Road, Rotherhithe, 1976. No picture in this collection conveys the borough's industrial decline so much as this one: a yard in the Surrey Commercial Docks which once belonged to the mighty shipbuilding firm of Harland and Wolff of Belfast is shown in ruins and desolation. The firm acted as contractors to the Port of London Authority. One of the more extraordinary tasks undertaken in that capacity was to repair Westminster Pier in 1926–7, after the whole pier had been towed downstream to Rotherhithe in November 1926. Harland and Wolff built HMS *Belfast* in the city from which the ship took its name (see page 124).

Tooley Street, 1967, showing Sun Wharf (left) and Toppings Wharf (right). Most wharves had arched windows of standard size, and openings or loopholes in a vertical line on both the river and land sides.

Bankside, 1977. This view is facing downstream (towards Southwark Bridge) and features the site of Sam Wanamaker's revived Globe Theatre on the right. The Globe's site, happily, had been owned by Philip Henslowe, the theatrical entrepreneur, early in the seventeenth century. The Jones-Willcox Patent Wire-Bound Hose Co. Ltd. was a part of the Willcox engineering firm, which had its main premises in Southwark Street. The firm occupied Nos. 47 and 48 Bankside, known as British Lion Wharf, from 1960 to 1976. By 1977, cargo-handling on the river had gone, and remaining industrial uses of riverside sites were few. Redevelopment has been drastic here in the past 20 years.

Bankside, 1971. This photograph was taken just a few yards farther upstream than the previous view, but six years earlier, and therefore it catches more vestiges of industry in the form of the riverside cranes. At one time, there were few parts of the riverside which were not used for handling cargoes, either directly from ships or from barges or lighters. The property on the right with the shield of arms is the residence of the Provost of Southwark Cathedral. It dates from the early eighteenth century. The next property along, No. 49, which juts out beyond Cardinal Cap Alley, has attracted many myths since 1945. It is an agreeable house dating from the beginning of the eighteenth century, which has fortunately survived when most of its neighbours have made way for commercial buildings, but it never had any links with Sir Christopher Wren or the other notables claimed for it.

The Angel Public House, Rotherhithe, seen from the river, 1960. The large commercial buildings in the background belonged earlier this century to Wilmott and Cobon, engineers, and later to warehousing firms, and were known as Platform Wharf. The wharf was built on the site of King Edward III's fourteenth-century moated mansion, which archaeologists have excavated in the past dozen or so years. The Angel is the earliest recorded public house in Rotherhithe. Until the Second World War it was the neighbour of numerous firms which repaired barges. The last barge-repairing firm in Rotherhithe, Charles Hay and Son, closed its business only in 1997.

The Angel Public House and Rotherhithe Street, 1963. This view is looking east towards the centre of old Rotherhithe. Cathay Street runs off to the right. The gate on the left leads to Rotherhithe Stairs, one of the many old watermen's stairs which were once an essential feature of the riverfront. In 1963, there was already a gap between the Angel and No. 41, but the houses beyond still stood. The London County Council destroyed them soon afterwards for no good reason. The flats on the right also went: they were built in 1903–5 in Braddon Street and Fulford Street. The tall chimney belonged to Gillman and Spencer Ltd., millers and warehousemen.

A plaque to commemorate Bryan Donkin and John Gamble, who first produced tinned food in 1811 at a factory on this site in Southwark Park Road, which is now occupied by Aylwin School. The firm of Donkin was a major one in Bermondsey in the nineteenth century. It removed to Chesterfield in 1902.

Sainsbury's depot at Running Horses Yard, Blackfriars Road, October 1950. The great firm of Sainsbury's has had a presence near Blackfriars Road since 1890, when a depot was opened in Stamford Street and Bennett Street. A large office block called Stamford House was completed in 1913. The firm still has its headquarters there today. (Sainsbury's Archives)

Grey and Marten Ltd.'s City Lead Works, Southwark Bridge Road, 1977. The firm had been established in 1833, and these works dated from 1880. There were once numerous lead works along the riverfront; shot towers were a feature of the skyline. This site is now occupied by the *Financial Times*: a good example of offices from the City of London superseding old industry in Southwark.

Borough Road, 1974. On the right there is an empty site which had been occupied by the tenement blocks known as Queen's Buildings, and before them by the Queen's Bench Prison, a well-known debtors' prison. Subsequent to this photograph, it was used to build the low-rise Scovell Road Estate. The large building in Borough Road itself, and another at the back of it with a prominent chimney, belonged to the firm of Day and Martin, blacking manufacturers: a rather Dickensian fact in a part of the borough which is closely associated with Dickens. The small, white-topped building visible in front of the large one was occupied by E.J. and A.T. Bradford, architectural sculptors. It was derelict for many years after the firm left, but it has been restored in the 1990s as part of an excellent private development which has added to the street some attractive properties in Georgian style.

M. Manze's eel and pie shop at the junction of Peckham High Street and Peckham Hill Street, 1979. Eel and pie shops were once numerous in the borough, and the name of Manze is a respected one in the trade. A few years ago, the Museum of London held an exhibition on the subject, which is a characteristic but generally unremarked feature of London life.

G. Austin and Sons Ltd., Peckham Rye, 1981. This famous furniture business, sited between Philip Road and Scylla Road, was closed on 5 November 1994, and the premises were demolished in 1995. As in so many cases, flats now occupy the site.

Shops in New Church Road, Camberwell, near the junction with Kitson Road, 1953. The great age of shops was at the end of the nineteenth century, but down to the 1960s, small shops generally flourished. The rise of supermarkets then diminished them. Greengrocers, dairymen, butchers and fishmongers all began to disappear from high streets and lesser streets. The Old Kent Road is an obvious example of the trend.

Housing in Southwark since the Second World War

Addington Square, Camberwell, 1971. This elegant enclave was
once under threat from redevelopment, but its future has long been
assured. It is incredible to think that so attractive a part of the
borough was ever considered for demolition, but that fate did
overcome Nelson Square off Blackfriars Road, which was arguably
a grander survival (see page 99).

No. 8 Grove Park, Camberwell, 1972. Known as Grove Hill House, this three-bay property was built in *c.* 1776–80 for Henry Smith, and originally stood next door to the mansion built by the famous physician, Dr John Coakley Lettsom (where Nos 9–12 now stand). These properties commanded an enviable hilltop position in the Camberwell of the late 18th century, when there was still open land to the south, towards the village of Camberwell. Lettsom owned his estate until 1812. Afterwards, more houses were built in Camberwell Grove and it became a regular street. Colonel Henry Smith commanded the Camberwell Volunteers in the early 1800s, and served as a Director of the Bank of England. Lettsom was Physician to the Volunteers.

The opening of Alder House, Alder Street, near Sumner Road, Peckham, by Alderman A.F. Crossman, Mayor of Camberwell, 22 April 1950. Although much publicity has been given to the problems of large-scale council housing estates of postwar Southwark, there were many small schemes which were far more successful.

George Brown, Deputy Leader of the Labour Party, opens the Acorn Estate, Peckham, 20 July 1963. To the right of George Brown is Harry Lamborn, who was then serving as Mayor of Camberwell and afterwards became the Member of Parliament for Peckham.

The Bonamy Estate, showing Rotherhithe New Road, 1973. This is one of the postwar estates whose life has proved short, for within a generation it was being rebuilt. It has always been the case that an estate is praised when it is new, and is considered inadequate or decayed in after years. The process has speeded up, for some large estates built in the 1960s and 1970s were widely reported as having considerable problems within a decade or so of their opening.

Bell House, College Road, Dulwich, 1952. This grand house was built for Thomas Wright, Alderman and Lord Mayor of London, in 1767–9. In the twentieth century, it became for a while the house of the Master of Dulwich College, but it is now a private house. Whereas the rest of the borough has seen drastic redevelopment since 1945, Dulwich Village has retained most of its Georgian and Victorian buildings, and in the centre of the village there are still many grand old houses such as this one. What is not widely known is that such houses once stood elsewhere in the borough, even near the Bermondsey waterfront. Dulwich has been preserved because of its ownership by Alleyn's College of God's Gift. The same pattern can be seen in, for example, the Walcot Estate at Kennington. Charities were very conservative owners.

Bell Cottage, College Road, 1972. This attractive weatherboarded house dates from the eighteenth century. Another cottage nearby, Pickwick Cottage, is named in allusion to the fictional retirement of Dickens's famous character. At the end of *Pickwick Papers*, its hero 'may still be frequently seen contemplating the pictures in the Dulwich Gallery, or enjoying a walk about the pleasant neighbourhood on a fine day'.

Nelson Square, Blackfriars Road, Southwark, June 1951. Very shortly, these Georgian houses were to be demolished to make way for a development of blocks of council flats. Percy Bysshe Shelley, the poet, had lived at No. 26, whose ground-floor windows are boarded up. These standard late Georgian houses, with arched doorways and blind arches over the first-floor windows, were part of a square which dated from about 1807–14 and which were designed by S.P. Cockerell. They had followed on from the opening of Blackfriars Bridge in 1769 and the laying out of Blackfriars Road. Part of the square was destroyed by bombing but most of it was intact in 1945. If ever a set of old buildings in the borough deserved to be preserved and cherished, it was this one. Its destruction was a particularly hideous blot in the record of postwar redevelopment.

Barlow Street, Walworth, 1963. This street was subsequently demolished, a fate it shared with so many others throughout the northern part of the borough. Charlie Chaplin lived in this street in 1891, when he was just two, according to the census returns of that year. It is the earliest definite record of him in Walworth, although he was almost certainly born nearby. He claimed to have been born in East Street, but no proof has ever been found.

Trafalgar Street, Walworth, 1963. Another photograph taken prior to redevelopment. This street formed part of the Rolls Estate, which comprised considerable tracts of land in Walworth, Camberwell and Bermondsey and which had belonged until 1961 to Lady Shelley-Rolls. She was the sister of Charles Stewart Rolls, the early aviator and motorist, who founded Rolls-Royce. Old working-class residential estates such as the Rolls Estate were numerous in the borough until the 1960s, when they became uneconomic. Much of the property ended up in the council's hands.

Hillingdon Street, Walworth, 1964. The land on the western side of Walworth Road was a part of the ancient estate of the Dean and Chapter of Canterbury, which was largely leased and developed by the Penton, Clutton and Brandon families between the seventeenth and the nineteenth centuries. The landownership of Hillingdon Street and John Ruskin Street was more fragmented than that of the streets to the north. Hillingdon Street, which was called Hill Street until 1892 (after Viscount Hill, one of the Duke of Wellington's commanders), was redeveloped in the 1970s.

Newington Lodge, Westmoreland Road, Walworth, 1969. This was formerly the workhouse for the parish of St Mary, Newington, which had been built in 1852. As this picture shows, its design was closer to that of a gracious Georgian terrace than to the Victorian barracks of popular imagination. If it had survived another generation, it would surely have been converted into flats. Workhouses were formally abolished in 1930, when the old Poor Law was wound up, but in this case and many other cases, their function remained unchanged under another name. Newington Lodge was a hostel for the homeless in its later years.

Newington Lodge just before demolition in 1969.

101

Gurney Street, New Kent Road, *c.* 1970. These old tenements were about to make way for the Heygate Estate. The population density of this corner of Walworth was very high earlier this century, on account of the considerable height of the tenements and the fact that they lined a great many streets in and near the New Kent Road.

The Heygate Estate, 1973. The Victorian tenement blocks which stood near New Kent Road were in a run-down and even horrific state by the 1960s. When they were demolished, a large estate of council flats replaced them. The estate took its name from Heygate Street which ran off Walworth Road: an unexceptional Victorian street. The estate was built by Laing's on the 12-M Jespersen system, a method of prefabrication. The fabric of the estate soon proved problematic, and huge sums of money had to be spent to correct defects and deficiencies. But the main criticisms must concern its social and economic aspects. Firstly, the estate turned its back on New Kent Road and Walworth Road, and the whole area lost any normal street pattern. Everyone prefers a front door on a regular street, even if that door is of a block of flats. Secondly, the megalomaniac nature of the scheme squeezed out so much economic life from the area: the planning brief in 1968 nonchalantly stated that six shops would replace 'about 90', and two pubs the previous five. Thirdly, the elevated walkways were a help to criminals, not to residents. Finally, the new Heygate Street, which has no pavements or access to properties on either side, is a bleak and dismal street which is an emphatic retrogression from what it replaced.

Boyson Road, 1967. This was largely removed to make way for the Aylesbury Estate. Its houses had long formed part of the Walworth Common Estate, which had belonged to the Vestry of St Mary, Newington, in the eighteenth and nineteenth centuries and then passed to the borough council. The tall terraced houses were built in the third quarter of the nineteenth century. The street was named after Ambrose Boyson, who was a local Victorian worthy.

Westmoreland Road. This road was once called Walworth Common, because it ran along the north side of a piece of open land which was later used for housing. In the nineteenth and twentieth centuries it has sheltered a street market which was second only to East Street's, but is now much diminished.

The beginnings of the Aylesbury
Estate, Walworth (in the foreground).

The building of the Aylesbury Estate, *c.* 1971. This huge estate on the eastern side of Walworth is a prefabricated or system-built estate which was commissioned in the 1960s to try to reduce the housing list swiftly and substantially. Laing's built it according to the 12-M Jespersen system. There were no tower blocks, but the very long blocks which were built go up to 12 storeys. Their length detracts from their height, which is in fact much greater than that of Victorian tenement blocks in Walworth. An opening ceremony took place on 11 April 1970. About 2,700 homes were completed to house some 10,000 people. The estate's name derived from Aylesbury Road, an innocent back street, and on that prompting the individual blocks took their names from villages in Buckinghamshire, which commentators have naturally considered an unfortunate contrast. For as soon as three years after the official opening, the estate had become the subject of regular articles on the theme of 'sink estates', and by the 1980s its reputation was as dreadful as any estate in England. The elevated walkways which ran through the estate aided robbers and burglars, and there were structural problems which led, for example, to extensive water leaks. Much money is now due to be spent on the estate to try to improve life for its occupants.

The Aylesbury Estate, 1973.

Albert Terrace, Gladstone Street, off St George's Road, 1977. The houses in this street and in neighbouring streets have managed to escape redevelopment. Yet similar houses in similar streets elsewhere in the borough were demolished. The nature of the houses' ownership and occupation was crucial to their survival.

Silver Jubilee decorations in Hayles Street near the Elephant and Castle, 1977. Note the silver foil wrapped round the lamp post. The properties in this street and some neighbouring streets belonged to Hayle's charity, an institution in Lambeth. Institutional ownership often preserved estates of old houses such as this one.

Amelia Street, Walworth, 1978. This is a view of the Pullen's Estate in the last years when it was intact. The Pullen family built tenement blocks and associated workshops in several streets in the late1800s. The tenements on the right-hand side of this photograph have since been demolished. The view faces Walworth Road and includes the former tower of St John's Church in Larcom Street. The tower was removed soon afterwards, but the church remains in use.

Abbey Street, Bermondsey, 1954. The gaps left by wartime bombing had not been filled by 1954. Prefabs were still very numerous. In the distance, Abbey Buildings can be seen at the junction with Tower Bridge Road. They had been built on part of the site of Bermondsey Abbey by a railway company at the beginning of this century. It is difficult to imagine that a view from this spot 500 years previously would have looked towards a church of the size of Westminster Abbey. St Saviour's Estate, named after St Saviour's Abbey, was subsequently built on the right-hand side of the street.

Monarch Buildings, Abbey Street, 1961. At the other end of Abbey Street from Abbey Buildings, there were more tenements. They have since been demolished. The vast majority of Victorian tenement blocks have gone in the past 40 years. These buildings stood very near the Star Music Hall, and opposite the Neckinger Leather Mills and the Drill Hall of the Bermondsey Volunteers and Territorials.

The living room of No. 11 in Block 5 of the Adams Gardens Estate, Brunel Road, Rotherhithe, October 1950. Views of domestic interiors are comparatively rare and are consequently very interesting, even if they are only 50 years old.

The kitchen of the same flat in October 1950.

Scenes & Settings in Postwar Southwark

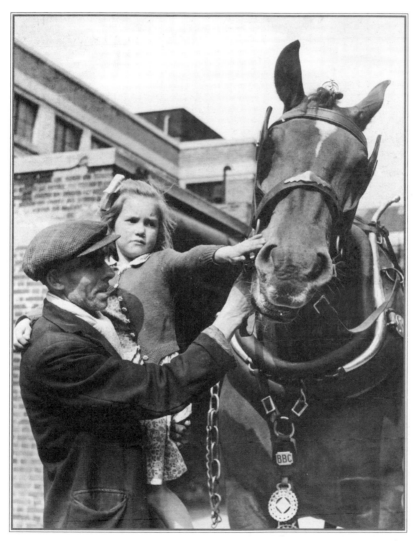

Linda Bladen and Henry Hewett, a driver, say goodbye to one of Bermondsey Borough Council's last horses, May 1953. It is surprising that this scene took place so late as the postwar years, for Camberwell Council has ceased to use horses in 1933. A few private commercial horse-drawn vehicles continued to appear in the borough's streets until the 1960s.

Bermondsey Borough Council's Stable Superintendent, Mr J. Page, and some of his drivers bid farewell to James, one of the horses made redundant in 1953.

Members of the Bermondsey Veterans' Club receive food parcels from the Alexander Miller Memorial Homes, Victoria, Australia, in the presence of Mr S.G. Carter, the Acting Agent-General for Victoria, 9 November 1950. Rationing still applied in England in 1950, and in the years immediately following the Second World War, a number of gifts were sent from Australia to groups in this borough.

Bermondsey Women's Club outing, 1954.

The opening of the children's playground at Tyer's Gateway, Bermondsey, May 1951. The Mayor of Bermondsey, Miss Eileen Greenwood, is seen in company with the directors of Barrow, Hepburn and Gale Ltd, the prominent local leather firm. They had provided the materials and equipment to transform the previously-derelict site.

A No. 68 tram photographed in Jamaica Road in June 1951. The route went from Waterloo to Greenwich. Notice the advertisement for the Trocette Cinema in Tower Bridge Road on the right.

The last tram, 5 July 1952. Trams were one of the badges of London in the earlier twentieth century, and their going in 1952 was a considerable change.

Robert Mellish, the Member of
Parliament for Bermondsey, greets
the crew of the last tram to leave the
Tooley Street terminus in his
constituency, July 1952.

Classes 1 and 2 from Albion
Primary School, Rotherhithe,
photographed on a school journey
to Sandown on the Isle of Wight,
1961.

The Trocadero, New Kent Road, November 1963. The great cinema at the Elephant and Castle was demolished the following year. Its Wurlitzer organ was preserved by the Cinema Organ Society and taken to the nearby South Bank University. One of the films advertised here is Alfred Hitchcock's *The Birds*, which was based on a short story by Daphne du Maurier.

The ABC Cinema, New Kent Road, Elephant and Castle, 1960. It has since been known as the Coronet. Entertainment on the site goes back to 1872, when the Elephant and Castle Theatre opened there with a performance of *Valentine and Orson*. The theatre was chiefly known for melodrama and pantomime. In 1930 it became a cinema. A plan to convert it into a church has been publicized in 1999.

Boxing Committee outing, 1949. The photograph
was taken in Wansey Street, Walworth, and the
building on the right was then the Town Hall of the
Metropolitan Borough of Southwark. Boxing was a
prominent sport at the nearby Manor Place Baths
down to their closure in 1978.

A view of Walworth taken from a tower block at the
Elephant and Castle, 1972. The railway line was
originally that of the London, Chatham and Dover
Railway, which was opened in 1862. To the left,
there is a coalyard which once belonged to the
London, Midland and Scottish Railway. Amelia Street
runs across the picture behind the signal box.
Beyond that comes Manor Place, which includes the
clock-turret and chimney of the baths which were
built for Newington Vestry in 1898. In the
background, on both sides of the railway, there is a
Council depot, which is still in use as a transfer
station for rubbish.

The Black Bull Public House on the corner of Old Kent Road and Bartholomew Street. Many people do not know that Old Kent Road continues on the north side of the Bricklayers' Arms junction for a short distance. This junction was its terminus; the main road continues as Great Dover Street. This public house is one of many which have disappeared in the postwar years. The fall in population, the decline of industry and massive redevelopment schemes all removed public houses, especially in the north of the borough. An unwelcome trend of very recent years has been the supersession of old names of some of the surviving pubs. This is one part of the borough's history which is often not noticed. For example, a pub called the Gibraltar stood in St George's Road, on the corner of Elliott's Row, because that vicinity was developed soon after General Eliott (sic) had defended Gibraltar in the great siege it suffered in 1779–83. The Gibraltar was renamed the Bedlam a few years ago and a piece of local history was discarded. Bartholomew Street recalls another piece of history: the ownership of the surrounding land by St Bartholomew's Hospital.

The Bricklayers' Arms road junction, photographed in 1963. The public house which gave the junction its name may be seen in the background, in the angle of Old Kent Road and Tower Bridge Road. On the left there is the Old Kent Road Library, which was a notable work of architecture. This junction was devastated by the megalomaniac floyover scheme of the late 1960s. The library, the public house, many agreeable old buildings and countless shops all disappeared.

Prizewinners at an open air art exhibition in Camberwell, 1951. The exhibition had been held on Camberwell Green.

A youth service in Havil Street, Camberwell, 1960. All those in this picture were members of uniformed youth organisations.

A road safety training scheme for young cyclists in Brunswick Park, Camberwell, 1959. The scheme was publicized in *Camberwell Calling*, Camberwell Council's newsletter.

Boy scouts distributing *The Queen's Highway* in Camberwell, 1955.

The opening of Lucas Gardens, Peckham Road, Camberwell, 28 July 1955. The gardens were named after Alderman J.F.W. Lucas, twice Mayor of Camberwell, who died in 1955. In this photograph, Alderman G.S. Burden, Leader of Camberwell Council from 1951 to 1960, stands second from the left at the front.

A festival gala at Lucas Gardens, Camberwell, 1959. The Mayor is Alderman Thomas Wallis (1959–60). Alderman G.S. Burden, Leader of Camberwell Council, stands on the right. Pearly kings and queens have long been a feature of local life, for the Old Kent Road and East Street have been centres for street traders or costermongers, from whose ranks the pearlies have come. They undertake charitable work and form a significant and interesting part of London's life.

The removal of a railway bridge across Lordship Lane, Dulwich, 1958. The spire of St Peter's Church, Dulwich Common, can be seen in the background. The bridge had carried the Crystal Palace line until its closure in 1954. The 1950s and 1960s were the nadir of the railways, when countless branch lines were closed.

The removal of tram lines outside East Dulwich Station, 1952. They had been there for fewer than 50 years, for Dog Kennel Hill had been widened for electric trams only in 1906.

Christmas film show for pensioners at the Odeon Cinema, Denmark Hill, Camberwell, 20 December 1955.

Nunhead Lane,1982. The prominent building with a clock-turret was formerly a garage for Banfield's coaches, which operated in the borough for many years in the middle of this century. Previously, from 1911 to 1919, it had been the premises of the National Steam Car Company Ltd., which ran steam buses. In recent years, there has been a campaign to try to save this building, and it has been decided to insist on its incorporation into any new development on the site.

The main gates of Nunhead Cemetery, Linden Grove, 1982. The inverted torches on the gate piers are symbolic of the extinguishing of life. The entrance gates and piers were designed by J.B. Bunning and were erected in 1840. The Anglican chapel at the top of the main avenue was designed by Thomas Little in 1844. Much restoration is due to take place here in the near future.

The monument of Thomas Tilling (died 1893) in Nunhead Cemetery, photographed in 1984. Tilling founded the famous firm of carriers and bus proprietors in Peckham and ran extensive premises there. He ran a regular horse-bus service between Peckham and the West End from 1851 and was the first to introduce double-deck motor buses to central London in 1904. The Bull Yard depot was the firm's first depot for motor buses in Peckham.

Boundary marks in Southwark Bridge Road, 1977. Before there were borough councils, there were civil parishes or vestries. In the 19th century, the vestries fixed small metal plaques to buildings to mark their boundaries. Here, at the junction of Southwark Bridge Road and Marshalsea Road, two plaques record the boundary between St George the Martyr Parish and St Saviour's Parish.

Guy's Hospital, 1988. This view is from the the open space known as 'the Park' and is looking towards Hunt's House and to Guy's Tower beyond. Originally, Guy's consisted only of the two quadrangles reached from St Thomas's Street. In the nineteenth century, the major addition was Hunt's House, which commemorated William Hunt, the hospital's greatest benefactor after Guy himself. Expansion of the hospital on land east of Maze Pond after 1945 led to Hunt's House being regarded as outdated, and it has been demolished in the 1990s. Guy's Tower was opened in 1975.

HMS *Belfast*, 1988. The ship is a cruiser, which was launched in 1938 in the build-up to the Second World War. Its principal armament consisted of twelve 6-inch guns, which fired 112 lb shells. The crew numbered 750–850. It saw action in the Battle of North Cape in 1943, in which it helped to sink the *Scharnhorst*, and again in the Korean War. It became a museum ship on the Thames in 1971, and ranks as a principal attraction to visitors in Southwark. Vast crowds turned out in 1999 to watch its return from an overhaul at Portsmouth. It is painted in wartime camouflage colours.

Hay's Galleria, 1988. This was the old Hay's Dock, which was filled in and roofed over and was considerably restored, in order to become an agreeable mixture of shops and offices in 1988. The huge sculpture in the centre, by David Kemp, is entitled 'The Navigators'. Hay's Galleria is the centrepiece of the first phase of a large redevelopment known as London Bridge City, which is a mixture of new buildings and of restorations of old ones. The entire site belonged to Hay's Wharf in the days of the upstream port. A second phase of redevelopment is due to take place at the eastern end of the old Hay's Wharf site, and will involve an office for the new Mayor of London.

Acknowledgements

Acknowledgement is gladly made to Mr Daniel Dougherty for his agreeing to my use of the picture of a class at Melior Street School on page 49; to Major J.M.A Tamplin TD for his kind permission to print the two photographs on page 28, of Lance-Corporal Keyworth VC and of the entry into Lille, which come from the archives of the Queen's (Southwark) Regimental Association; to Sainsbury's Archives and to the Company Historian, Bridget Williams, for permitting the use of the picture of Tress & Co.'s premises on page 35 and of the view of Running Horses Yard on page 92; to the late Cyril Bustin, who provided several pictures of pre-war Bermondsey, especially of the Bermondsey Gospel Mission, of which he and his wife were sometime Joint-Superintendents; and to Mr Charles Rumbold for the use of pictures from his excellent survey of Bermondsey in 1976. Most of the remainder of the illustrations belong to the Southwark Local Studies Library and are used by kind permission of Mr Len Reilly, Local Studies Librarian.

I would also like to thank Dr Peter Renton for sending useful information on synagogues; Mr Stuart Rankin for much help on matters maritime relating to Rotherhithe; Mr John Beasley and Mr William Marshall for sharing their considerable funds of knowledge on Peckham; and to Mr George Murfitt for valuable information on aspects of industry and transport before 1939. Opinions expressed in the introduction and in captions are of course my own.